APRIL

S	M	T	W	T	F	S
	1	2	3	4	5	
7	8	9	10	11	12	13
14	15	16	17	18	19	20
21	22	23	24	25	26	27
28	29	30				

D0636431

MAY

S	M	T	W	T	F	S
			1	2	3	4
5	6	7	8	9	10	11
12	13	14	15	16	17	18
19	20	21	22	23	24	25
26	27	28	29	30	31	

JUNE

S	M	T	W	T	F	S
						1
2	3	4	5	6	7	8
9	10	11	12	13	14	15
16	17	18	19	20	21	22
23	24	25	26	27	28	29
30						

CONTENTS

Benediction .... Iris Hesselden
Snowscape .... Kathleen Gillum
Nuts In Winter .... Ian Nimmo White
Breath Of Spring .... Kathleen Gillum
On The River: A Canadian Memory .... Peter Cliffe
A Moment Of Magic .... Katherine S. White
Tender Memories .... Kathleen Gillum
The Way They Came .... Kenneth C. Steven
The Lover .... Glynfab John
Daybreak .... Kathleen Gillum
Touch Of Spring .... Elizabeth Gozney
Waiting .... Peter Cliffe
May Morning .... Glynfab John
Cottage Garden .... Kathleen Gillum
Bluebells .... Brian Gent
Butterflies .... Teresa Kelly
Free Spirit .... Kathleen Gillum
Grandfather .... Katherine S. White
Silver .... Walter de la Mare
Sundial .... W. Blacklaw
Where Bluebells Grow .... Stanley C. Gordon
A Humble Pleasure .... Kathleen O'Farrell
Northumberland .... Iris Hesselden
Anemones .... M. Munro Gibson
Simple Things .... Kathleen Gillum
Out-Of-Season .... Maurice Lindsay
Skye .... Kenneth C. Steven
An Evening Stroll .... Alison Mary Fitt
September Heat-Wave .... Brenda G. Macrow
Reflected Views .... Glynfab John
Swallows .... Kenneth C. Steven
Cumbrian Picture .... Iris Hesselden
Crystal Butterfly .... Kathleen Gillum
Nocturne .... Brenda G. Macrow
The Potato Pickers .... Kenneth C. Steven
Apples On October Trees .... Glynfab John
Dawning Of The Day .... Kathleen Gillum
Softly Eventide .... Elizabeth Gozney
Carsebreck .... Kenneth C. Steven
October Days .... Kathleen Gillum
November .... Iris Hesselden
Winter Approaches .... Kathleen Gillum
From A Railway Carriage .... Robert Louis Stevenson
Freedom Of The Sea .... Regan Smith
Winter Delights .... Kathleen Gillum
Lovers' Gate .... Glynfab John
I Name This Child .... Alison Mary Fitt
Winter .... Regan Smith
King Winter .... Kathleen Gillum
Prayer .... Katherine S. White

The Fireside Book

A picture and a poem
for every mood
chosen by

David Hope

Printed and published by
D.C. THOMSON & CO., LTD.,
185 Fleet Street, LONDON EC4A 2HS.
© D.C. Thomson & Co., Ltd., 2001.
ISBN 0-85116-782-9

BENEDICTION

SITTING quietly, doing nothing,
   I leave the troubled day,
Sometimes thinking, often dreaming,
The world seems far away.
Sometimes hearing music playing,
Softly all around,
Sometimes only breezes blowing
Fill my head with sound.

Sitting quietly, doing nothing,
Serenely by myself,
The seasons change, the Spring
  returns,
The grass grows by itself.
Nature gives her benediction,
Gentle peace within,
Sitting silent in the twilight,
Feel the peace begin.

Iris Hesselden

SNOWSCAPE

LOOKING out on distant hills
  All clothed with white on white,
I marvel at the depth of snow
That's fallen overnight.
Fields once like a patchwork quilt
Of varying shade and hue,
Underneath a lacy shawl
Lie hidden now from view.

The atmosphere is crisp and chill
And has an icy nip,
The mosaic of the countryside
Is held in Winter's grip.
Trees look skeletal and stark
Against the Wintry sky,
A lonesome bird in morning flight
Lets out a plaintive cry.

I see the spire of the church
The school, the village hall,
And houses dotted here and there
All hidden by snow fall.
The scenes that once seemed
  commonplace
Familiar to the sight,
Have been transformed and
  turned into
A dazzling world of white.

Kathleen Gillum

NUTS IN WINTER

ONCE they had concluded that
  The intruder was no sharply
Angled or robotic man-made cat,

They shot from off the garage roof
And garden wall to where it hung
Yard-armed on the hairy birch, quite safe:

An unplanned gathering of clans,
A tartan; of acrobatic tits,
Coquettish chaffinch, cautious robins,

Greenfinches with their pugilistic jabs.
Within the hour they'd sussed
The need for order, with three drab

Branches, parallel, deft rungs
Of a ladder where they filed,
Like choir boys ruffed-up for song.

In turns they'd thrust and parry
The wires on this fast food diner,
Until the unwatched light had slipped away.

Ian Nimmo White

BREATH OF SPRING

TODAY I caught upon the breeze
The first sweet breath of Spring.
A murmuring throughout the trees
A thrush began to sing.
Some tiny snowdrops I did spy
So fairylike and small,
And crocus cups have caught my eye
Beside the garden wall.

How delicate the primrose is —
She shows her dainty face
Amongst the spears of daffodils
Which jostle for their place.
With bud and blossom breaking forth
On every hedge and tree,
Whilst birds are busy building nests
With great activity.

New foliage is on every branch
In verdant shades of green,
The leaves are lush and fresh and new
And have a special sheen.
Spring brings a sudden surge of life
Pulsating through the earth,
Awakening all the dormant things
And bringing them to birth.

Kathleen Gillum

ON THE RIVER:
A CANADIAN MEMORY

I SAW it pass by, a canoe on the river,
Moving downstream at the close of the day.
A breeze from the hills made the slow waters shiver,
And the long grass was cool on the bank where I lay.

Above the dark forest the sunset was burning,
And the play of their paddles could scarcely be heard.
Intent on their journey, their heads never turning,
The man and his woman spoke never a word.

Carried afar on the cold river's flowing,
As in a deep dream, they were borne from my sight;
But I murmured 'Bon voyage! Where'er you are going,'
Then returned to my camp in the hush of the night.

Peter Cliffe

A MOMENT OF MAGIC

THE car purred homeward through the dusk
In the half-light that lends a strange magic.
Across the loch, the village winked
In the inky distance.

Like statues, the deer stood in the roadside stream,
Poised on slender legs, still as the night.
It seemed they hardly breathed.
Four lovely creatures. Silhouetted.

The car slowed and drew level
Before they came to life
To flit away and melt into the trees,
Into a violet dark.

Katherine S. White

TENDER MEMORIES

AS sunshine filters through the trees
Creating a design,
The tracery of lacy leaves
Is delicate and fine.
And dappled patterns on the path
Of sunshine and of shade,
Will vanish with the evening dusk
When light begins to fade.

And when the wind goes dancing by
And whispers in the trees,
It stirs up thoughts of earlier days
And tender memories,
When you and I were first in love
And walking hand in hand,
All starry-eyed you told me of
The future you had planned.

Today it seems all cool and fresh
With green and growing things,
Whilst overhead upon a bough
A speckled song-thrush sings.
Just walking through this leafy lane
Of calm tranquillity,
Has opened for me once again
The gates of memory.

Kathleen Gillum

THE WAY THEY CAME

WHEN he got a tune
   It just came
Glanced off the fiddle
As if a skiff of breeze
Had caught the bow.

Just that first phrase
In the middle of nowhere;
As he was shearing sheep
Or cutting peats.
A few notes
That maddened his head
Like bees till he'd caught
them.

His eyes listened,
At an angle, all night,
Wanted silence
As if the other notes
Were out of reach,
Close, a swarm nearing
His fingers' hive.

In early morning
Always, the tune lay,
Born, beautiful,
Living, like a child —
The father fast asleep.

Kenneth C. Steven

THE LOVER

HE dreams
Of unromantic things:
Of sparking plugs
And piston rings;
Of carburettors
And cylinder heads;
Of clutch plates, valves,
And twisted threads.
Her bonnet
Lures him from afar,
His true love
Is — a motor car!

Glynfab John

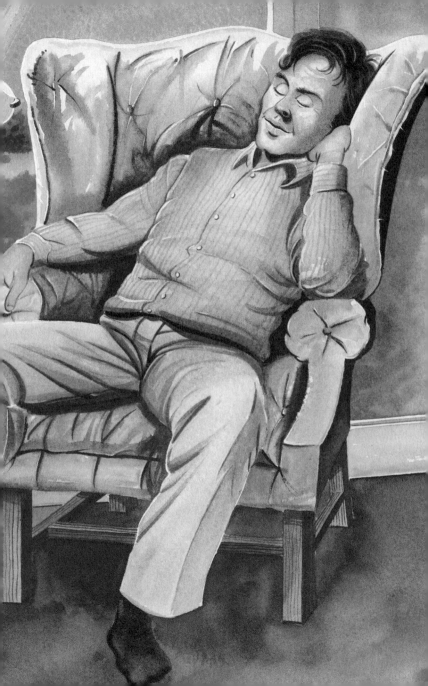

DAYBREAK

WITH the breaking of the dawn
The velvet shades of night,
Are drawn back like a curtain
The earth is washed with light.
The sky is flushed with colour
The clouds are tinged with gold,
The sun comes up and smiles upon
A world that's tired and old.

Subtle scents and secret sounds
Are mingled in the breeze,
The fluttering of feathered wings
Wind whispering in the trees.
With dew still wet on petals
There's fragrance in the air,
As morning spills a rosy glow
Of radiance everywhere.

The atmosphere is cool and fresh
Bathed in tranquillity,
There is a sense of peacefulness
And quiet serenity.
It's in this early stillness
As darkness steals away,
A blush of beauty falls upon
The birthing of the day.

Kathleen Gillum

TOUCH OF SPRING . . .

By mossy banks where violets grow,
And clouds of bluebells dance away;
Where primrose constellations flow
To greet the brightness of the day.
Where cuckoo flutes his timeless call,
And crowned in pink, the clover's eye;
Through flurry of the blossom's fall
By murmur of the breeze's sigh.
Where dappled sunshine smoothly spills
In burst of golden rays, to bring
A radiance to the distant hills,
By order of delightful Spring!

Elizabeth Gozney

WAITING

HIDES the sun behind the mountain,
  Sad the gulls cry o'er the sea;
Cool the breeze and soft its whispers:
You are coming here to me.

Red and gold the sunset lingered;
Darker now is heaven's blue;
Shadows are the night's own children,
Watching as I wait for you.

Colder now the wind and stronger;
Loud the waves march up the strand.
Life's the road that lies before us;
Love is all we understand.

Down the path I see you hasten,
Guided by the bright star-shine;
Long the waiting, sweet the greeting,
As your hands reach out for mine.

Peter Cliffe

MAY MORNING

I WANDER where dew-drops
Glisten like diamonds
In the golden-ringed,
Morning-size light;
Where the larkish air
Is delicately laced
With the invisible
Threads of song;
Where blossom-wise May
Foams over the hill,
And the breeze wears
The perfume of Spring.

There, a silver-voiced stream
Cadenzas its way
Through the arias of
Rhythmic-ferned moss;
The warmth of the sun
Is a God-natured prayer,
And the trees leaf
A green benediction;
On a mattress of grass
Earth-bedded I lie,
With the skytide
Of blueshine above me.

Glynfab John

COTTAGE GARDEN

A COTTAGE with a roof of thatch
  With casements opened wide,
A flagstone path that twists and turns
With urns on either side.
Where spears of blue delphiniums
Are standing tall and bold,
And honeysuckle tendrils wind
Their trumpets pink and gold.

The foxgloves nod their dainty bells
'Midst sage and rosemary,
As grasses whisper in the wind
Swaying gracefully.
The hollyhocks and lupins give
A colourful display,
And poppies stand in flimsy dress
In beautiful array.

Butterflies with tinted wings
And droning honey bees
Are visiting the lavender,
Cornflowers and sweet peas.
With rambling roses tumbling down
Around an old stone well,
This seems a place quite magical
And holds me in its spell.

Kathleen Gillum

BLUEBELLS

HOW delightful when one sees,
  Bluebells growing 'neath the trees,
Their lovely azure misty haze
Brings memories of childhood days,
When eager little fingers would
Pick as many as they could,
Carried home at end of day,
A bruised, bedraggled blue bouquet!

Brian Gent

BUTTERFLIES

BUTTERFLIES are flying flowers,
With their petal-soft touch
They bless the bowers.

In their satin and velvet vestments
They perform the rites of Spring,
Recreating fragrant beauty
With nectared, pollen-powdered wing.

You flutter by
O butterfly,
Take me with you, please!
But like a sigh you disappear
Into the honeyed Summer breeze.

Teresa Kelly

FREE SPIRIT

BEAUTIFUL creature flying free
You span the earth and sky,
With light upon your feathered wings
Forever soaring high.
Dipping and diving with the wind
And gliding through the air,
Wheeling and weaving in and out
Free bird without a care.

Skimming the surface of the sea
Your wings just tip the waves,
Then up on to the craggy cliffs
To rest in hidden caves.
Each movement seems so effortless
Performed with skill and grace,
I watch with awe your agile form
Just drifting throughout space.

And as I look at your display
I feel my spirit rise,
My heart leaps up and wants to fly
With you in sunny skies.
Worries and cares drop from my mind
I lift my head up high,
Inspired by this enchanting bird
Whose playground is the sky.

Kathleen Gillum

GRANDFATHER

HIS two hands held my upturned face,
The brown eyes beaming into mine.
We crossed the generation leap
And recognised the myth of time.

The child I was looked back in love,
In awe, in pride — and swiftly knew
That something in our searing gaze
Held more than kin between we two.

It bound me close despite the years,
Held me fast and made me know
That something in him burned in me,
Though I would stay and he would go.

Katherine S. White

SILVER

SLOWLY, silently, now the moon
   Walks the night in her silver shoon;
This way, and that, she peers, and sees
Silver fruit upon silver trees;
One by one the casements catch
Her beams beneath the silvery thatch;
Crouched in his kennel, lIke a log,
With paws of silver sleeps the dog;
From their shadowy cote the white breasts peep
Of doves in a silver-feathered sleep;
A harvest mouse goes scampering by,
With silver claws, and silver eye;
And moveless fish in the water gleam,
By silver reeds in a silver stream.

Walter de la Mare

SUNDIAL

STRAIGHT as a silent sentinel I stand,
A pivot on the lawn. This is my place.
Though not akin to all who circle me
I warmly fraternise with those at hand
Who share my world and pass the time of day
Until the blazing orb has run his race.
I bear no buds, yet breathe a simple charm
Of grey antiquity amongst the green.
And as the green blends slowly with my grey,
I follow Nature's eye, that she may lean
Her lengthening burden on my offered arm.

W. Blacklaw

WHERE BLUEBELLS GROW

SPIDERS' webs like lace are spun,
Bedecked with amber dewy pearls,
Glinting in the misty, morning sun,
As the light of day unfurls.

In a dell, where bluebells grow,
Fox cubs scamper, roll and play,
Disturbing pheasants as they go,
Screeching, fleeing from the fray.

Beside a copse, the tinkers camp,
Tent frames made from supple willow.
Reed matting keeps out cold and damp.
Heather forms a perfumed pillow.

Ripples lap the lochan shore,
Where forget-me-not and daisy bloom.
Gulls gather there, by the score.
Sparrows chirp amongst the broom.

Church bells chime across the vale,
Sounding clear and ringing long,
And as daylight turns to pale,
People stroll to evensong.

Stanley C. Gordon

A HUMBLE PLEASURE

HEADY with joy, I enter this small world,
  This fragrant place, enclosed so charmingly
By walls of crimson damask, dewdrop-pearled,
Satiny-smooth, and cool as ivory;
This honeyed haven, with its glorious sheen,
Stirring so gently, when soft breezes blow,
Set in dark foliage, red against the green,
Where velvet butterflies flit to and fro.
Oh me, oh my, what sheer and utter bliss,
That toil should be as pleasurable as this!

A little, brindled bee, one may suppose,
Might have such thoughts, were he the lucky one
To find a glowing, sweetly-scented rose,
Just opening to the sun . . .

Kathleen O'Farrell

NORTHUMBERLAND

The Kingdom of Northumbria,
A very special place,
A land of mellowed villages,
Of moors and empty space.
A country steeped in history
Where past and present meet,
From windswept Roman fortress
To vibrant city street.

On river bank or by the sea
The ancient castles stand,
And Bamburgh, still magnificent,
Keeps watch across the sand.
The wide expanse of earth and sky
Will tempt you back one day,
And beautiful Northumberland
Will steal your heart away!

Iris Hesselden

ANEMONES

COME," she said
"See the anemones."
We stood in the frame of her back window,
Looking on green, green grass, birdbath;
Graceful Silver Birch, twig frail, slimly strong,
Rising above tidy borders
And the small pointed neatness
Of several evergreens.

A gentle scene in the good clear light
Of this mid-January day,
Afternoon sky streaked with gold . . .
But I had not expected to see anemones.

She must have dreamt them.

But suddenly, nestling in a crevice
Among some white rocks, I saw
Pink, purple, mauve anemones . . .
A minute cluster of hope.

M. Munro Gibson

SIMPLE THINGS

THE fragrant scents of Summer
A blue soft-pillowed sky,
The gentle whisper of the wind
As it goes trembling by.
The dew still wet on roses
The hum of fluffy bees,
The interplay of light and shade
Amongst the poplar trees.

The golden notes of birdsong
The tints on magpie wings,
And gossamer of spider webs
All seem such simple things —
And yet they hold much beauty
Design and artistry,
As nature yields her secrets
For those with eyes to see.

Kathleen Gillum

OUT-OF-SEASON

GONE are the happy children, shouting splashes
Along the castled sands of Summer's beach.
Now, the frustrated lip-curled ocean lashes
The vacant shore; throws wrack beyond its reach.

Folded away the ice-cream vendor's awnings,
The trampoline upon the esplanade;
Empty the old folk's shelter, where the fawnings
Of sunny breezes warmed them in the shade;

Pipe-smoking old men holding poles as handles
To hook huge draughts across a tarmac board;
The print-dressed shoppers, gym-shoed or in sandals,
Asking bright windows what they should afford.

Now, gusts of rain sweep sauntered streets and shutters
That front closed boarding-houses and hotels;
Sharp hailstones lash their hard staccato stutters
From winds that swirl away the seaside smells
And all the easy trail of Summered leisure,
Fiercing survival on this place of pleasure.

Maurice Lindsay

SKYE

BURNS talisker from the hills
And pools run dark as pure cairngorm.

The bracken is turning the colour of foxes
The air burns with the scent of peat.

The Atlantic combs the coast, white and wild,
Loud birds steer the high wind.

Up on the ramparts of the Cuillin
An eagle is flying at half-mast.

Kenneth C. Steven

AN EVENING STROLL

As Dave and I go strolling
Down our avenue,
When dusk is deeply rolling
There is a warming view
Through windows, bright and glowing,
Of families having tea,
While old Sam's slowly going
To sleep in number three.

There's Nancy busy knitting
By the fire in number eight,
While next door Jim is sitting
With his newest girlfriend, Kate.
I love the dress she's wearing,
It's silky at a glance —
I wouldn't say I'm staring,
Just notice it by chance!

Of course, Dave says I'm nosy
But I have to disagree —
I just like to see folk cosy
In their houses, so you see
I find it quite spell-binding
To glimpse what's going on
When daylight is unwinding,
And curtains aren't drawn!

Alison Mary Fitt

SEPTEMBER HEAT-WAVE

WARM days of leisure, sweet surprise,
 These timeless hours ere Summer dies —
A pause before the Autumn breeze
Steals golden treasure from the trees.

No hint of frost, no thought of death —
It seems that Summer holds her breath
And heeds our plea to stay awhile
And charm us with her lingering smile.

The dewy fields of stubble bare
Wear gold tiaras in their hair;
The sea is calm, the air is sweet,
And sands are warm beneath our feet.

As in a time-warp, roses red
Forget their velvet gowns to shed —
Such precious hours, however brief,
Before the falling of the leaf!

Brenda G. Macrow

REFLECTED VIEWS

SOFTLY, gently,
Like falling dew,
A new awareness
Within me grew

As shining peaks
Dissolved in light,
And silver lakes
Flashed, mirror-bright

Until my eyes
Were dazzled by
Reflected views
Of earth and sky.

Glynfab John

SWALLOWS

ALL Summer they are there above us
  Playing games with the air
Voices that fill the breeze
Day after blue day.

Until one morning they are gone, flown south,
The grey dusky left pale and empty —
In every lane that's softened up with leaves
The death of Autumn.

How many thousand miles
Lie mapped in the handful of each swallow?
A whole ocean of journey, an Africa
Planned and perfect in these wings.

All Winter I will wait at the window of my world
To welcome them once more.

Kenneth C. Steven

CUMBRIAN PICTURE

BEYOND the wide-world's end
This picture will remain,
Of Cumberland in Autumn,
Each fellside, tarn and lane.
The shadows on Blencathra
That change from mauve to grey,
The cottage lights in Caldbeck
That brighten fading day.

The golden bracken on the hills,
The trees in glory dressed,
A gentle mist in Borrowdale
As red sun paints the west.
The early frost that touches
Tells Summer to be gone,
Beyond the world, but in my heart
This picture lingers on.

Iris Hesselden

CRYSTAL BUTTERFLY

SUSPENDED from the ceiling
Upon a fine mesh chain,
A fragile crystal butterfly
Rests by the windowpane.
It's carved just like a diamond
Of delicate design,
Each facet catching sunbeams
That glint and gleam and shine.

A sudden flash of colour
Rays of prismatic light,
From pink to blue then amethyst
Brilliant, dazzling, bright.
They burst and bounce across the walls
Like jewels in the gloom,
And leave a host of tiny rainbows
Dancing in my room.

Kathleen Gillum

NOCTURNE

IN the fire-gold evening
   The crimson sun has died;
The last frail rays are leaving
Deep glen and mountainside.

Long fingers on the ocean
Trace lines of liquid light —
The only sign of motion,
Wild geese in arrowed flight.

The purple islands darken
Against the creeping shade,
While glowing eyes awaken
In copse and woodland glade.

The cold moon sheds her radiance
Upon the waters deep —
Withdrawn in realms of silence,
The hooded mountains sleep.

Brenda G. Macrow

THE POTATO PICKERS

HOLLOWS of mist; September smells so thick
Of chestnuts scudded down and leaves in wet
And water drumming choked towards the town.

Farms lie here, dark as blackened books,
And dykes rib over chests of curving land
Into the rain.

Like fish creels crates are steepled
There by the field's edge. Slumped with mud
The tractor's rumbled track reflects the sky.

Now the pickers splay down in the ruts,
Thudding their baskets with pale lumps
All out of shape and smooth as fossil shells.

They move like ragged crows across the day,
Legs planted wide, heads slanted over rain
Until in bleary stars lights home the dusk.

Kenneth C. Steven

APPLES ON OCTOBER TREES

APPLES on October trees:
  Glowing in the mellow rays
Special to Autumnal days —
Not a potentate of old
Boasted jewels bright as these!
Falling leaves of green and gold
Gathered by a gentle breeze,
Drifting through the balmy air,
Leave them gleaming, hanging high,
Gems against a velvet sky!

Apples on the orchard trees —
Every grey and lichened bough
Shows its harvest treasure now:
Never did a Grecian maid,
Dawdling in Elysian shade,
Pick such fruit, so sweet and fair,
Ripe with sun, and warm to hold:
Did she breathe a scent so rare?
Luscious and how tempting these
Apples on October trees!

Glynfab John

DAWNING OF THE DAY

NIGHT stands waiting in patient pose
  In robes of ebony,
Glittering stars within her hair
Winking mysteriously.
With the keys of day in her hand
She gently unlocks the dawn,
And draws back a velvet curtain
Revealing a blushing morn.

    Rays of rosy pink and cream
    Stream out across the land,
    As if a jug of liquid light
    Was spilt by unseen hand.
    The world is draped in pastel shades
    The sun begins to rise,
    All clothed in golden garments
    Which flood the morning skies.

        Scarlet and amber, mauve and peach
        With pearl and silver hints,
        A canvas worked by artist's brush
        A tapestry of tints.
        The sombre beauty of the night
        Steals silently away,
        Her darkened veils are vanishing
        With dawning of the day.

Kathleen Gillum

SOFTLY EVENTIDE . . .

WHERE smooth the waters flow,
  And evening brings the tranquil hour of calm;
Where pastures lush, encroach upon the shore,
Protected by the rising sweep of hills.
This place now holds its own nostalgic charm,
And through the trees, the dappled sunshine spills —
A burst of glory, 'ere the shadows grow,
And dusk begins to dominate and draw
A misty veil across the waning light,
Till darkness folds its mantle o'er the night . . .

Elizabeth Gozney

CARSEBRECK

WE drummed the car door shut and stood
Looking over a place under bluest water.

A sudden curlew rose up crying,
Dripping a necklace of broken pearls.

We pushed through pools that lipped our ankles
As the swans flowed over their flooded land.

A reed bunting nodded on a flute of grass
Was blown away by a bit of breeze.

The geese came scrawling in from nowhere,
Skidded on water and squabbled over grass.

And the sun rose jagged from the world's rim,
Drenched us in soft and orange fire.

Kenneth C. Steven

OCTOBER DAYS

OCTOBER brings the morning mists
A haze of silver light,
Shrouding garden, hedge and tree
She hides them from our sight.
And as she dances through the woods
A magic wand she waves,
Transforming all the countryside
Into October days.

A time when all the Autumn leaves
Are falling from the trees,
And smell of woodsmoke in the air
Is carried on the breeze.
When squirrels busy hoarding nuts
Dart nimbly to and fro,
Building up a hidden store
Before the Winter's snow.

The golden fields at harvest time
Are ripe with corn and maize,
Ready for the gleaner's hand
In these October days.
The world is splashed with vivid things
Now that October's here,
This really is a lovely month . . .
A special time of year.

Kathleen Gillum

NOVEMBER

NOVEMBER fog now
   drifts and blows,
November daylight
   swiftly goes,
And moving on the
   motorway
Car headlights
   pierce the fading day.
Wet mud lies round the
   farmyard gate
Where patient sheep all
   safely wait,
The grey-black trees
   stretch out their arms
And shelter distant,
   fire-lit farms.

The countryside has
   settled down
And Winter holds
   each field and town,
November creeps
   across the land
And touches with his
   chilling hand.
Yet far beneath the bare,
   grey earth
New life, new seeds
   await their birth,
And as November plays
   his part,
New thoughts of Spring
   grow in each heart.

Iris Hesselden

WINTER APPROACHES

AN icy hand has crept upon
   The earth without a sound,
There's frost upon the furrowed field
And on the fallow ground.
For Winter is approaching
There's a tingle in the air.
The trees have long since shed their leaves
And stand there stark and bare.

Their branches intertwine and weave
A fragile filigree,
And trace an intricate design
In pearl and ebony.
The rooks encircle vacant nests
Then disappear from sight,
As curls of woodsmoke rise and merge
In watery Winter light.

A solitary old stone church
Stands out in silhouette,
Against the background of the sky
Forlorn it seems and yet —
Light streams from diamond window panes
And voices start to sing —
The year is coming to its end
But there is hope of Spring.

Kathleen Gillum

FROM A RAILWAY CARRIAGE

FASTER than fairies, faster than witches,
Bridges and houses, hedges and ditches;
And charging along like troops in a battle,
All through the meadows the horses and cattle;
All of the sights of the hill and the plain
Fly as thick as driving rain;
And ever again, in the wink of an eye,
Painted stations whistle by.

Here is a child who clambers and scrambles;
All by himself and gathering brambles;
Here is a tramp who stands and gazes;
And there is the green for stringing the daisies!
Here is a cart run away in the road
Lumping along with man and load;
And here is a mill, and there is a river:
Each a glimpse and gone for ever!

Robert Louis Stevenson

FREEDOM OF THE SEA

I'll join your moonraking crew, my lad,
To sail through the dancing foam
And feel the wind blowing through my hair
As I turn my back on home,
Then I'll learn the freedom of the sea
With just the ship, the wind and me.

When we heave her to in strange ports, my lad.
Let us not tarry too long,
Let's set her sails on the turn of the tide
To the tune of an old sea song,
For I yearn for the freedom of the sea
With just the ship, the wind and me.

To the top of the mast I'll climb, my lad
Keep watch in the high crow's nest
I'll scale the rigging, reef the sails
And bend my back with the best,
Then I'll feel the freedom of the sea
With just the ship, the wind and me.

In the heat of a calm I'll bask, my lad,
'Til the south wind fills her sails,
And when tides rip beneath her keel
I'll fight the Winter gales,
Then I'll know the freedom of the sea
With just the ship, the wind and me.

On a night black sea I'll steer, my lad,
By the light of the stars above,
In the silent watches I'll be free
For this is the life I love,
We'll roam the seven seas forever
The ship, the wind and me together.

Regan Smith

WINTER DELIGHTS

ON copper pots and polished brass
  The lamplight glints and gleams,
Giving out a steady glow
And shedding golden beams.
The fire blazing in the hearth
And flickering of flames,
Casts shadows on the ceiling
Which dance in ghostly games.

Rows of books like well-loved friends
Reach out to welcome me,
As I sit in my chintzy chair
With cup of steaming tea.
With cushions made of tapestry
And rugs upon the floor,
This cosy room with old oak beams
Feels comfy and secure.

The wind is moaning eerily
With Winter in its train,
And snow is falling steadily
Beyond the window pane.
As curtains drawn against the dark
Screen out the Wintry night,
This hour of sweet contentment
Is savoured with delight.

Kathleen Gillum

LOVERS' GATE

LEAN on this weatherbeaten gate,
Five-barred of oak, and strong,
And while we linger, until late,
Ask: Has it been here long?

How many lovers of the past
Have dallied in this way,
And wished the bloom of bliss would last
For ever as in May?

Did they court here in days gone by,
And dawdle, hand in hand,
And by this gate, like you and I,
Did they in Springtime stand?

Did they at hawthorn blossom stare,
And kneel where bluebells mass,
And did he gently stroke her hair,
And kiss his shy young lass?

Grey-lichened now but sturdy yet,
Dry hinges stiff with rust,
Will Lovers' Gate, where we have met,
Still creak when we are dust?

Glynfab John

I NAME THIS CHILD

UPON this day your downy head
Is sprinkled, while your name is said,
And standing with you at the font
We pray it is a name you'd want.

For on a name we pondered long,
We didn't want to get it wrong
Nothing too obscure or clever
For you'd be stuck with it forever!

Something very trendy? No,
For fashions come, and fashions go
A family name might well be good
But that can start a family feud!

If only you could wait 'til grown
And be allowed to choose your own,
But, little one, you had no say
In the name you have today.

So we wish you joy and health,
Happiness, contentment, wealth,
And hope that you will like your name
If not, you'll know who to blame!

Alison Mary Fitt

WINTER

There's fury in the crashing tide,
 Bleak menace in the countryside,
Wild rivers race, gales scream and rage,
The world is trapped in Winter's cage.
Birds cease to sing, proud trees stand bare,
Soft swirling snowflakes fill the air,
As desolation shrouds the land
Frost paints the earth with brittle hand,
'Til one March morn clouds creep away,
A golden sun adorns the day
And now with joy though blackbirds sing
Do we yet dare to welcome Spring?

Regan Smith

KING WINTER

KING WINTER taps an icy wand
Upon my windowpane,
I rise to glimpse his dazzling form
Go dancing down the lane.
He wears a shimmering mantle
And robes of sparkling white,
He scatters silvery snowdust
Into the inky night.

And with his breath he blows into
The tingling atmosphere,
In velvet sky the shivering stars
Are twinkling bright and clear.
And thrusting frosty fingertips
Into the cold still air —
A million crystal shining shapes
Lie glittering everywhere.

And where he's skipped with tinselled feet
The hoary frost appears,
And once-green grass of garden lawn
Has turned to frozen spears.
With icicles like glinting gems
Adorning bush and tree,
He leaves his icy signature
For everyone to see.

Kathleen Gillum

PRAYER

WHEN twilight blue begins to fall,
    When puss-cat slips along the wall,
When no-one passes by at all,
Leave a little chink for me.

When wind is rattling on the pane,
When streetlamps glimmer in the rain,
When thoughts come crowding round again,
Leave a little chink for me.

When darkness hurries down at night,
When raging storm is at its height,
When someone draws the curtains tight,
Please —
Leave a little chink for me
To see.

Katherine S. White

The artists are:—

Sheila Carmichael; Daybreak,
May Morning, Cottage Garden,
Simple Things, Apples On October Trees.
Jackie Cartwright; Waiting,
An Evening Stroll, I Name This Child.
John Dugan; Butterflies,
Softly Eventide . . ., Freedom Of The Sea,
King Winter.
Val Fraser; Nuts In Winter.
Alan Haldane; Skye, October Days,
Winter.
Eunice Harvey; Tender Memories,
Touch Of Spring, Anemones,
Crystal Butterfly.
Harry McGregor; Breath Of Spring,
Out-Of-Season, September Heat-Wave.
Norma Maclean; Benediction,
Grandfather, Where Bluebells Grow,
The Potato Pickers.
Sandy Milligan; On The River :
A Canadian Memory,
The Way They Came, November,
Lovers' Gate.
Keith Robson; Snowscape, Sundial,
Northumberland, Reflected Views,
Cumbrian Picture, Dawning Of The Day,
Winter Approaches,
From A Railway Carriage.
Staff Artists; A Moment Of Magic,
The Lover, Bluebells, Free Spirit, Silver,
A Humble Pleasure, Swallows, Nocturne,
Carsebreck, Winter Delights, Prayer.

JULY

S	M	T	W	T	F	S
	1	2	3	4	5	6
7	8	9	10	11	12	13
14	15	16	17	18	19	20
21	22	23	24	25	26	27
28	29	30	31			

AUGUST

S	M	T	W	T	F	S
				1	2	3
4	5	6	7	8	9	10
11	12	13	14	15	16	17
18	19	20	21	22	23	24
25	26	27	28	29	30	31

SEPTEMBER

S	M	T	W	T	F	S
1	2	3	4	5	6	7
8	9	10	11	12	13	14
15	16	17	18	19	20	21
22	23	24	25	26	27	28
29	30					